A Jagdtiger is an impressive sight, even after the self-demolition charges go off. Note the small brackets in the centre top of the glacis, the tow shackle hanging from the base of gun travel lock, and the 'Pilze' on the top edges of the superstructure. The plate over the driver/radio operator's position has ruptured out of position, flipping the conduit for the headlight, and the engine deck is off. The tiny hatch in the foreground is the belly escape hatch which was located under the radio operator's position, and is a detail not usually seen. This photo had the tag line *"4984 HQ-A2-14 April 1945. Calvano."* T/3 S. Calvano, of the 165th Signal Photo Co., also took the picture on page 38 of *Panzerwrecks 3* of Lt. Col. Miller in Obernetphen, Germany, holding a 12·8cm round on 9 April 1945. **USAHEC**

Self Destruct: Story of a Jagdtiger

Self Destruct: Story of a Jagdtiger

Per Martin Block: The location has only recently been confirmed as being at the Brakeler Strasse in front of the since-demolished Glashüttenwerk at Bad Driburg, east of Paderborn, Germany. The 'Y' marking leads to the assumption that it belonged to 2./s.Pz.Jg.Abt.512. The 1. and 2. Kp. each received 10 Jagdtigers and ended up in the Ruhr pocket. Therefore, the location makes it more likely that it belonged to the 3. Kompanie outfitted with just 7 Jagdtigers, which went from Paderborn towards the Harz mountains. Date of loss should be 2 April 1945. The gun travel lock is still attached, so it is reasonable to assume the vehicle broke down and was destroyed by the crew. The attached towing cables reinforce this theory. The light coloured ammunition is HE (Spr.Gr.L/5,0) and the dark coloured is AP (Pz.Gr.43). **Pages 4-5:** Close-up front and rear. The texture of the mantlet and details of the gun travel lock are notable. **4x USAHEC**

Self Destruct: Story of a Jagdtiger

Opposite: A view of the 'Fliegerdrehstütze 36' fitted to the Jagdtiger's engine deck hatch. The small clips at the very top of the mount needed to be changed to fit either the MG34 or MG42. Firing back on attacking aircraft with tracers, however blindly, helped to dissuade pilots from pressing home their attacks.
Left: The massive breech block of the 12·8cm Panzerjägerkanone 80 L/55 is missing its handle. The gunner would have sat to the left of the gun. His sight is long gone, but the armature for it remains. The elevation handwheel can be seen under the armature. **Above**: A soldier poses for his photo and allows us to see more of the left hand side of the vehicle. It has been noted that the skirt mounting brackets haven't been welded on in a straight line on either side, a sign the quality control was nose-diving at the Nibelungenwerk in St. Valentin, Austria, the assembly firm.

2x USAHEC, 1x L.Archer

Self Destruct: Story of a Jagdtiger

Pages 8-10: A Panzerjäger Lr.S für 7·5cm Pak 40/1 lies on a roadside near Hesdin, France, its fighting compartment wrecked. It was photographed by Major A G Sangster, an intelligence officer in the Canadian Army. He noted: *"... a hole in the superstructure which suggests a penetration by HE. The vehicle was burned and badly damaged by the explosion."* We would not disagree, as one half of the fighting compartment has been blown away, and the remainder of the thin armoured plate is peppered with small holes, particularly visible in the above photo and on page 10. Hans Weber kindly gave us his thoughts on who might have used this little SP gun: *"The Marder I at Hesdin I put to 348 Inf. Div. The unit was on the Channel Coast since mid August 1944 between the Somme estuary and Boulogne. It moved Southeast towards Cambrai on a route that Hesdin is on starting August 31st 1944. Likely that the movement was interdicted by Jabos."*

3x LAC

This 4·7cm Pak (t) (Sfl.) auf Pz.Kpfw.35 R 731 (f) was knocked out by a Canadian manned PIAT near Antwerp, Belgium. Examining the damage are L/Cpl. G.H Hawkridge & Spr. WE Rea.

NARA

Two Polish soldiers look over a destroyed Panther Ausf.G in Germany in 1945. The hand painted style and location of the tactical number, and style of track hangers on the turret side, lead Roddy MacDougall to believe that we are looking at a vehicle from Pz.Rgt.16 or 24 from 116.Panzer-Division. In this view we can see the bracket for an 'Orterkompass' in the centre of the turret roof and the driver's and radio operator's hatch plate precariously perched on the glacis, behind the climbing soldier. See *Panzerwrecks 5*, page 15 for another 116.Panzer-Division Panther lost in a similar area of Germany.

PISM

Some rear end details such as the 'Flammenvernichter' mufflers with welded armour guards and roadwheels with their tyres burnt away. The tank was probably pushed to its location off the side of the road after it had lost its track, as it has left ruts in the earth. Furthermore, it could be argued that the broken and burnt roadwheels and missing track are linked. Maybe it was hit in the running gear and, facing capture, was disabled by the crew setting off demolition charges. Two explosive charges were carried, one in the fighting compartment, one in the engine compartment to disable the vehicle. This would set off the stowed ammunition - which is enough to lift the turret.   **PISM**

Top left & right: Two photos taken by a British Army photographer showing the details of the 'chin' mantlet, The track hangers were welded to the turret side after the tactical number had been applied. Roddy McDougall observed that the large circular marks on the face of the mantlet are casting plugs left over from the casting process, the horizontal marks being left after they were milled to an acceptable tolerance. Note the casting number and 'YMK' on the front plate. **Left:** A more general view of the wreck. It ended its days at the Sennelager training ground before being scrapped. There was no special name given to the 'chin' manlet by the Germans: the only distinction was the part number changing from '5255' for the normal mantlet to '5258' for the 'chin' mantlet.
2x TTM, 1x PISM

Roddy MacDougall points out that this Panther Ausf.G *"... was assembled by MNH probably after February 45, it has the later engine deck installed by MNH with the same size of fuel and coolant armoured caps. This engine deck also has the later armoured cover made with three welded flat plates in the vertical pane as opposed to a single curved armour plate."* The placement of the tactical number is unusual, as is the fact that someone has failed to take the road wheels, despite removing the nuts. Features to note are the hoops to tie down foliage on the turret sides and the hole in the turret roof in front of commander's cupola to allow a steel tape to pass through to connect an I/R sight to the gun. **AMC**

A rear view of 15cm Panzerwerfer 42 left in its Dunkelgelb (RAL 7028) photographed somewhere in Germany by a Royal Artilleryman. Possible unit identities are Volks-Werfer-Brigade.7, 8 or 9 as they ended the war in Western Germany. Another possibility is Nebel-Lehr-Rgt.2 from the Nebel-Truppen-Schule in Celle near Hannover. **RA Museum**

A Gleisketten Lastkraftwagen 2t, offen (Maultier) Ford Baumuster V 3000 S/SSM (Sd.Kfz.3b) lies wrecked on a roadside in Germany. The remains of the cab show it to have been fitted with the later 'Holzfahrerhaus,' although much of this is missing, along with one side of the cargo bed, the engine cover and the front wheel. **USAHEC**

Instead of having his subject stand in the sunlight for his picture, the photographer had him pose in the shade by a sun dappled Sturmgeschütz III Ausf.G to add a bit more interest. In doing so, he has done us a favour, as we see how well the StuG blends into its surroundings. Now imagine you were an Allied tanker, and you had to cross that field in the background... This vehicle has the 'Rundumfeuer' MG mount on the roof and a coax MG in the 'Topfblende'. A small section of 'Schürzen' protects the side pannier. **L.Archer**

This photo was taken in Herbach, Germany by Max Berger, a forward observer with the 65th Armored Field Artillery Battalion in November 1944. Per Timm Haasler: *"In the morning of 5 October elements of 30th US Inf Div started to attack against the German line Herbach-Merkstein and managed to capture several bunkers. Around noon elements of Kampfgruppe Schrader (Grenadier-Regiment 148 and StuG.Brig. 902) started to counter-attack. At 6.30 p.m. Herbach was back in German hands again. The Germans reported one StuG III of StuG.Brig.902 lost."* This Ausf.G has a welded mantlet, steel return rollers, and its gun is out of battery.

P.Johnson

Prepared for a recovery that never came, this MNH assembled Jagdpanther G1 is from Nov-Dec 44 production having the ventilator over the gun in the front centre of the roof! It has foliage loops on its sides, glacis and mantlet as well as being necklaced around the break in the sectional gun barrel and behind the muzzle brake. This was a rare field modification rather than a factory application. The vehicle has the 110mm tall guards over the periscopes, angled port side tool stowage and lacks the 'Pilze' sockets on the roof. All hatches on the roof and engine deck are open, and the crescent plate over the gun sight protrudes over the edge of the roof. **Inset**: A more comprehensive view. **2x MIM**

The same Jagdpanther (with the tactical number '233' now visible) photographed by Maj W H J Sale, MC, 3rd/4th County of London Yeomanry (Sharpshooters) who gave the location as "south of Cleve," which points toward 2./s.H.Pz.Jg.Abt.655. Martin Block shared this information with us: *"The embankment in the background could have been the Kleve-Goch railway. The s.H.Pz.Jg.Abt.655 supported 84.Infanterie-Division during the initial defence of the Reichswald starting on the 2 February 1945 and then counterattacked Kleve from the south with the 116.Panzer-Division parallel to this railway on the 12th. The 2./Pz.Lehr-Rgt.130, with new Jagdpanthers in its second company, arrived in Marienbaum on the 18th and was engaged more to the southwest in the Kalkar - Uedem area the next day."*

NAM

Another MNH Jagdpanther G1 with relocated ventilator and another failed recovery. The hard edged camouflage scheme with its striking contrast indicates it was built on or after November 1944. The earth may have ploughed up when they tried to tow it or, failing that, the stricken and scorched vehicle may have been cannibalised and dug in. The location is believed to be Frankfurt am Main, where fighting started around 25 March 1945 in the face of the US 6th Armored Division driving northward, with the Rhein-Main airfield as the likeliest setting. The Frankfurt area would point toward s.H.Pz.Jg.Abt.519 as being the unit. The tube for the gun tube cleaning rods lies twisted in the foreground.

1x USAHEC, 1x W.Auerbach

'Sarge' Bealko Shoots a Tiger II

A photo of a Tiger II from ETO Ordnance Technical Intelligence Report No. 35 dated 16 October 1944. Observations by 1st Lt. George D.Drury, Ord.Tech.Intell Unit 'E' attached to First US Army. Two Tiger II's were examined: Fahrgestell Nummer 280101 and 280105. The bulk of the report dealt with type and stowage arrangement of the sixty-nine rounds of 8·8cm ammunition carried. The vehicle already has the number '1034' painted on the glacis. The broken right track trails off in the distance. **Opposite page:** The 8·8cm Kw.K has been removed from Tiger No. '113,' and a portion of the interlocking glacis plates has been cut out with a torch.

1x NARA, 1x D.Trowbridge

'Sarge' Bealko Shoots a Tiger II

This Tiger II, from 1./s.SS-Pz.Abt.101, was lost during a rearguard action at Avenue du Maréchal Foch near the junction of Rue de l'Industrielle, in Jemappes (2km west of Mons) while acting as a roadblock to safeguard the retreating German troops against advancing US troops. It was lost in the night 2nd / 3rd September 1944, when it ran out of fuel and was abandoned by its crew. G.Davison and G.Bosch are on the tank facing us.   **1x D.Trowbridge, 1x E.Bealko**

According to Uscha. Werner Wendt, when the company was re-equipped with Tiger II in early August 1944, the commander was Oscha. Fritsche. Whether Fritsche was still in command of the tank on 2 September is not known. The tank was towed from the Avenue du Maréchal Foch to the location where the majority of our photos were taken. Here Ed Bealko's buddies, T.Crisalle, Staten Island, NY, G.Bosch, Sioux Center, IA, and G.Davison, Salem, OR, from the 18th Tank Battalion, 8th Armored Division, look over the Tiger.

E.Bealko

'Sarge' Bealko Shoots a Tiger II

Opposite: All the 'Zimmerit' has been stripped off the glacis. Other fittings and sheet metal items are also missing, leaving us an unadorned hull and turret to inspect. Ed 'Sarge' Bealko took these photos in Mons, Belgium, in October, 1945.

Above and right: 'Legs' Bernstein, all six foot of him, poses in front of the Tiger's track. '1034' was the number applied by an Allied survey team. See pages 74-85 for Panzer IV/70 (V)s assigned numbers '1032' and '1037.' It seems the chunk of nose armour has been quite carefully cut away.

Far right: G.Davison poses with unidentified buddy, probably G. Bosch. The unit insignia for s.SS-Pz.Abt.101 is visible next to the left exhaust pipe but the 'Balkenkreuz' has been totally obliterated. The belly of the beast lies on the ground.

4x E.Bealko

'Sarge' Bealko Shoots a Tiger II

'Sarge' Bealko Shoots a Tiger II

Additional views of the rear of the vehicle, with and without its main armament. Notice the pronounced overhand of the turret when traversed to the side. The photo on the far left apparently shows the tank while on the Avenue du Maréchal Foch. **Far left:** Chalked on the right mudflap, *"Il y a des explosifs à l'intérieur."* (*"There are explosives inside."*)

1x E.Bealko, 2x NARA

Several detail photos from the Intel Report. Of particular interest is the screening over the engine air intake. While the circular exhaust fans are covered by 2mm diameter wire on a 20mm grid, the square mesh over the air intakes is 6mm wire on an 18mm grid, the same heavy mesh used for the 'Drahtgeflecht-Schürzen' (wire mesh skirts) on late war Pz.Kpfw. IV Ausf.Js. Note the engine deck hatch is secured by lock down strips with a bolt in the centre.

4x NARA

A photo from the estate of Grover Schinbeckler, a member of the 82nd Airborne, taken outside the kiosk in the Hunnerpark on Sint Jorisstraat, Nijmegen, around 18-20 September 1944. The GIs are standing with a veteran of the early campaigns, a Pz.Kpfw.II Ausf.b with Ausf.F idler, possibly from Fallsch.Pz.Ers.u.Ausb.Rgt. HG. The small (open) hatch at the end of the engine deck is a unique feature of the Ausf.b. The hatch for the radio operator, also open, is visible directly in front of the clock in the background. When swinging the turret in free traverse, the commander would have to take care not to trample the r/o, who sat very close by, facing backwards. The small hole was for the antenna mount.   **L.Archer**

Another antique Pz.Kpfw.II Ausf.b, albeit incomplete and smoking. Either the turret has been blown off, or more likely it was a 'Fahrschule Fahrzeug' or Munitions-Panzer, a fate that befell many an obsolete AFV. The time frame was probably Autumn/Winter 1944/5 judging by the way the GIs are dressed. Note the armored division patch on the left sleeve of the young GI staring at the camera.

L.Archer

S/Sgt. Gennaro 'Jerry' Servedio of the US 751st Field Artillery Battalion photographed Mike Defillipo leaning against the remains of a Sturmgeschütz III Ausf.G near Neuhof, Germany in September 1945. Martin Block takes up the story: *"There is a town called Neuhof some 15 km SSW of Fulda. This would fit into the area of operations of Pz.Ausb.Verb. Thüringen. On 31.3.1945 it had reported 4 unspecified StuG with H.Pz.Gren.Feld-Ausb.Schule Wildflecken."*

P.Servedio

A catastrophic explosion has caused this Sturmgeschütz III Ausf.G to break apart. The superstructure has parted company with the chassis, losing its roof and side wall in the process. The wreck was photographed by a soldier in the 1st Polish Armoured Division. Note the Sd.Kfz.10/5 in the background and the Panzerfausts under the gun of the Sturmgeschütz.

PISM

These photos, of the same Sturmgeschütz III Ausf.G, were taken by Charles Chapman of the 69th Infantry Division whose caption stated *"Tiger Tank. In woods near Autobahn, Höneback, Germany. July 1945."* Martin Block fills in the blanks: *"There is a village called Hönebach some 30+ km west of Eisenach. This would fit into the area of operations of Pz.Ausb.Verb. Franken. On 1.4.1945 it had a.o. reported 6 StuG III with Pz.Ausb.Abt.1, 1 StuG III with Pz.Ausb.Abt.7 and 18 unspecified StuG with Pz.Lehr-Abt. Bergen/Fallingbostel."* A note about colour: After 'Zimmerit' was dropped, everything was painted at the factory. The dark colour on the StuG seen here, produced in November-December 1944, was the red primer undercoat, as instructions were to paint less that half the vehicle in a camouflage colour. All paints were applied very thinly. **2x C.Chapman**

Above: The same StuG from the previous pages, although the photo is from another collection. **Opposite:** Mr Chapman also photographed a second StuG in Hönebach, and it looks as though its tooth has fallen out. It also has a nonstandard method of mounting 'Schürzen,' but here the brackets along the track guards appear fixed, whereas the wing nuts present on the brackets along the track guards on pages 36 and 37 indicate those brackets were adjustable, possibly to accommodate the wider 'Ostketten'. In both cases, the upper brackets look to be tack welded to the superstructure sides, which would have weakened the armour.

1x USAHEC, 1x C.Chapman

39

A 'G.W.II für le.F.H.18/2 (Sf.) 'Wespe' found at Hillersleben, a German Proving Ground for testing artillery and artillery rounds. Why this normal SP gun was there is unknown, as any standard 10·5cm piece could have been used.

USAHEC

The 'Wespe' was a very compact vehicle. Note details of driver's hatch and adjustable bars on the front for carrying spare track. The vehicle is completely devoid of any markings or camouflage, not even a 'Balkenkreuz' is present.

USAHEC

Wa.Pruf. reserved several Panther Ausf.Ds to use as test beds, and this example, with 1943 era tracks and weights installed in place of the turret, is one of them. The bowed-out drive sprocket capped by an armoured cover held in place by four bolts was Part No. 48395 designed for the Ausf D and A but seldom seen mounted. (See *Panzerwrecks 3* page 93 for a photo of this armoured cover on a Jagdpanther but with twice as many bolts in the tooth ring.) Photo said to be taken in Germany near 'Garmish' around March 1945 by Daniel H Talt, 55th Armored Engineer Battalion, Engineering Recon Platoon. Garmisch-Partenkirchen is probably the location referred to in his caption.

D.Talt

This Bergepanther Ausf.A, covered in 'Zimmerit' from nose to tail, has features of the Ausf.G, such as extensions on the spade and modified tool stowage. Note that the tow cable is anchored at a point directly above the forward 'C' clamp, as on the Ausf.G, and two additional 'C' clamps are located further back on the hull side. Pulleys and other equipment fill the winch compartment. The wooden sides of the 'bridge' above the superstructure were hinged to fold down, but the front and rear portions were 'staked' so as to be removable.

D.Brown

Oldtimers at Schmalnau

The photos on pages 44 - 49 were received from August. Holz, a veteran of 'C' Company, 311th Infantry Regiment, 78th Infantry Division.

A GI from C Co., 311 Inf., 78th Div. poses in front of a rather forlorn Pz.Kpfw.IV Ausf.C found, according to the notation on the photo, in Schmalnau Germany. Note the armoured cowl for the coax MG. The side armour of 14·5mm would have kept out his rifle rounds but little else that was flying around in 1945. Between the two cracks in the superstructure is a band of paint where the antenna trough was once located. The first road wheel has the larger hub cap, indicating it was designed for the wider tracks introduced with the Ausf.E. It looks as though a faint number '6' was painted in front of the radio operator's visor.

Timm Haasler initially thought the Panzer III's and the Panzer IV belonged to HUS Eisenach which had a mixture of 13 old Panzer III and IV's in its inventory in 1945. Schmalnau - Ebersberg fit into the general area where the unit fought. Martin Block considered that Schmalnau, some 15km SSE from Fulda, on the other hand, would fit the area of operations of Pz.Ausb.Verb. Thüringen. He goes on to say: *"On 31.3.1945 Pz.Ausb.Verb. Thüringen had a.o. reported 7 unspecified Pz. III with Pz.Ausb.Abt. 300, 2 unspecified Pz. IV with H.Pz.Gren.Feld-Ausb.Schule Wildflecken. In MS#B-360 O. Munzel, CO Pz.Ausb.Verb. Thüringen, states that H.Uffz.Schule für Pz.Schtz. Eisenach arrived on 29./30.3.1945 with 3-4 unspecified tanks.*

So Pz.Ausb.Verb. Thüringen is a good guess although not 100% confirmed."

A.Holz

The same vehicle, but this time the caption claims the photo was taken in Simmerath! The 311th's sister regiment, the 310th, swept through Simmerath in early February 1945 prior to the 78th Inf.Div. capturing the Schammenauel Dams, but we've already established a stronger case for Schmalnau. (Had the photos been received separately however, we might have had problems with the unit identification.)

The heavy contrast camouflage scheme seems to be composed of four colours. Note the patches of a lighter shade of paint along the bottom edge of the 'Zusatzpanzerung.' A photo like this can prove instructive: The normal 30mm thick armour on the hull front was not face hardened. When it was decided to uparmour the Pz.Kpfw.IV, a standard package was issued to the troops that contained a 30mm face hardened armour plate for the hull and two 20mm curved strips of normal armour that could be welded on to hold it in place, thus increasing protection but adding considerable weight to the vehicle as well. The cut outs on the bottom corners accommodated bolts that secured internal components (final drive/brakes).

A.Holz

Oldtimers at Schmalnau

Oldtimers at Schmalnau

This page and opposite: Picasso would be proud of this one! Pz.Kpfw.III No. '132,' with its 'Gepäckkasten' on the ground behind it, appears to be an Ausf.F (note the bottom hinged cap for the starter crank in the centre of the rear armour plate). If so, it underwent a program of rearmament, uparmouring and suspension strengthening with many upgraded components and improvements: the front return roller has been mounted further forward nearer the shock absorber; its main armament is a 5cm Kw.K L/42 instead of a 3·7cm Kw.K; it has the newer commander's cupola but the older turret rear, sloped at 25°, and an armoured cover protects the smoke grenade rack.

2x A.Holz

Oldtimers at Schmalnau

Oldtimers at Schmalnau

Tank number '131' is a Pz.Kpfw.III Ausf.G that had also been cycled through the Waffenamt's rearmament program. It was retrofitted with 30mm of additional armour bolted to the hull front and across the driver's front plate, spare track stowage across the bow, modified suspension, spare road wheels on the track guards, and a 5cm Kw.K instead of a 3·7cm Kw.K. (Full details of this 'Umbewaffnung Programm' can be found in *Panzer Tracts No.3-2*.) Note also the 'Mittelstollen' (a spring loaded ice cleat that snapped into the middle of the track link) inserted in the mounted track, the AA MG mount on the turret roof, and the cannon barrel snapped like a matchstick. Sunlight catches the edge of the opened hull escape hatch.

A.Holz

A Pz.Kpfw.III Ausf.J minus its idler and armoured side visor for the gunner. (You can see the original colour around the edges of the cutout.) Note how the broken track drapes between the return rollers.

A.Holz

Oldtimers at Schmalnau

Left: S/Sgt Jack Kitzerow, a cameraman with 1st Infantry Division, looks at a broken German rifle on 20 April 1945. He stands next to a late production s.Zg.Kw.18t (Sd.Kfz.9). Amidst the detritus, next to the halftrack, is a box of grenades.

NARA

Right: A schwere Zugkraftwagen 12t (Sd.Kfz.8) photographed in Strasbourg, France, by Sgt. T/4 William Toomey of 3rd Signal Co., 3rd Infantry Division. The US personnel are from 10th Engineering Combat Battalion and are seen loading explosives into the halftrack. The plan was to fill it with 6000lbs of explosives and ram it into one of the triangular ring of forts near Mutzig that protected Strasbourg. **Below:** This photo, retouched by the US Army, shows the halftrack behind a smokescreen to obstruct enemy observation on 5 December 1944. Ultimately it failed to detonate and mortars were used to set it off, leaving a 15 foot hole in the fort's wall.

1x USAHEC, 1x D.Toomey

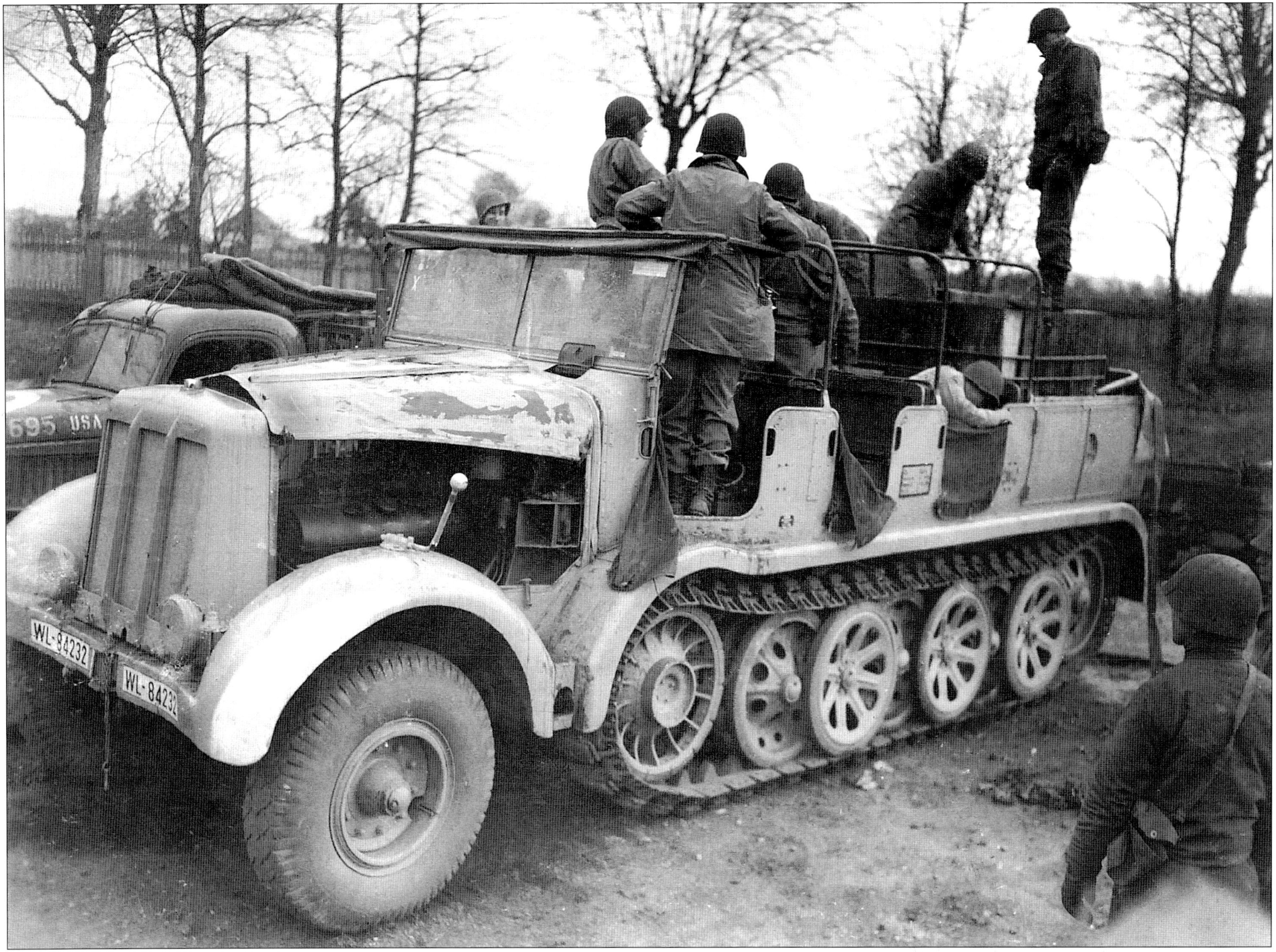
695 USA
WL-84232
WL-84232

A schwere Zugkraftwagen 12t (Sd.Kfz.8) at war's end. The castle seen in the background on the left could be the Burgruine Kropfsberg, Achensee, Austria, where most of 17.SS-Pz.Gren.Div. surrendered. The photos are from a fellow named Eddie Tyson, who was a sergeant in the anti tank company of the 222nd Infantry Regiment, 42nd Infantry Division. According to Shelby Stanton's indispensable *Order of Battle, US Army World War II*; the 42nd "...passed through [Munich] 30 Apr 45. The division then cut across the Austrian border north of Salzburg on 5 May 45 where it was located when hostilities were declared ended 7 May 45."

B.Gauthier

The twelve tonner could be found in many formations but normally served as a prime mover for artillery. The rear stowage lockers held tool boxes and accessories such as snow chains. At the very rear would be the tow coupling and connection for the air brakes as well as payout for the winch cable. Our GI seems to be taking aim at something behind the 'Sitzkasten' where normal stowage would be for the 'Mannschaftgepäck' and rifles. A vehicle jack would be stowed under one of the seats.

B.Gauthier

Mittlerer Zugkraftwagen 8t (Sd.Kfz.7) with 'Pritschen-Aufbau.' Note the squared off track guard. The end wall of the crew seat has a rounded, rather than a bevelled, edge. This vehicle has been 'winterised' because the two square covers between the front fender and track guard covered ports for the transfer of heated engine coolant, and the small lugs in the middle of the bumper held the auxiliary starter crank. Normal tool stowage included a shovel and pick axe on the engine cover, both absent here. Note the shutters on the radiator.

Eddie Tyson, the vet who took these photos, loved posing in comical poses on armour and guns. Another veteran who knew him mentioned that he remembered "babysitting" fields of German armour while waiting for the war to end. We can only say that, comical or not, the photographs offer us a glimpse of vehicles in Austria we might never have seen otherwise, and we are fortunate to be able to present them here.

B.Gauthier

Flakwagen - late war style. The same GI sits in the gunner's seat of a 2cm Flakvierling 38 on the cargo bed of an Opel Blitz 3,6-6700 A. The guns sit low on their normal ground mount and could depress another 10°. The folding sides of the cargo bed have been recycled from another vehicle, as we can clearly see the stripes and bolts on the side, and the top slats are missing all around. The large bin below the cab appears to be a field mod as well. Next to it are a pair of quad and single 2cm Flak guns and a 7·5cm le.I.G. Per Martin Block: *"On 1.4.1945, 17. SS-Pz.Gren.Div. had reported having eighteen towed 2cm Flak, including one 'Vierling,' and fourteen 7,5 cm le.I.G. 18/37."*

B.Gauthier

Flak guns surround a S.Pz.Sp.Wg. (Fu) (Sd.Kfz.232) (8 Rad) that has no armament of its own. The Flakwagen on the previous page is behind it - note the barrels and cab. 'Scharnhorst' has managed to outlive most of the reconnaissance cars that left the factories after it, and one wonders if it was through the cunning of its crew or just sheer luck. Either way, our GI doesn't care, it's just a playhouse to him. The ID of 17.SS-Pz.Gren.Div. is confirmed as the SS-Pz.Aufkl.Abt.17 surrendered in the Inntal near Münster and Jensbach. It was the only Panzer unit in the sector likely to come into contact with the 42nd Inf Div. The 222nd Rgt of 42nd Inf Div was to be stationed at Jensbach from 15 May 1945.

2x B.Gauthier

These two views offer a wealth of detail. At the far edge of the page is the antenna base for the 'Sternantenne,' also visible in the inset photo on the previous page.

2x B.Gauthier

A captured American M8 Armored Car, known as a Panzerspähwagen M8(a), has been converted to take a M.G. 151/15, although only one barrel remains. Some interesting details emerge the longer you look at the photo, such as the tactical number '342' and (unknown) unit insignia on the turret, and the guard rail fitted around the engine deck much like that fitted to a Sturmgeschütz. The gunner's head and torso would have been dangerously exposed when in action. **Above:** The gun mount was bolted and braced to the turret.

2x NARA

The PSW was covered in ETO Tech Intell report No.351 dated 17 July 1945. Observations by Lt. J.F. Eppes and Pfc. W.F. Wilcock, Ord. Tech. Intell. Team No.15. *"The normal 3·7cm gun was removed from the turret and a steel plate welded in the rear or the turret 8 inches below the top thus forming a shelf to which the triple machine gun mount was bolted. Each side of the mount was braced by a rod welded to the top of the turret. The guns are mounted so that the barrels extend over the rear of the turret. In ordinary use the turret is traversed 180° so that the guns point to the front of the vehicle. The normal 360° traverse is retained and the gun has free elevation."*

NARA

Pz.Kpfw.35 R versus Allied firepower. Although not certain, it is believed that the following photos show former Pz.Kp.224 tanks under the command of Pz.Jg.Abt.657. The obliterated back end gives a unique view of the Pz.Kpfw.35 R and its Renault 4 cylinder engine. The plate on the ground is the cast rear plate, its lower edge being closest to the camera.

2x LAC

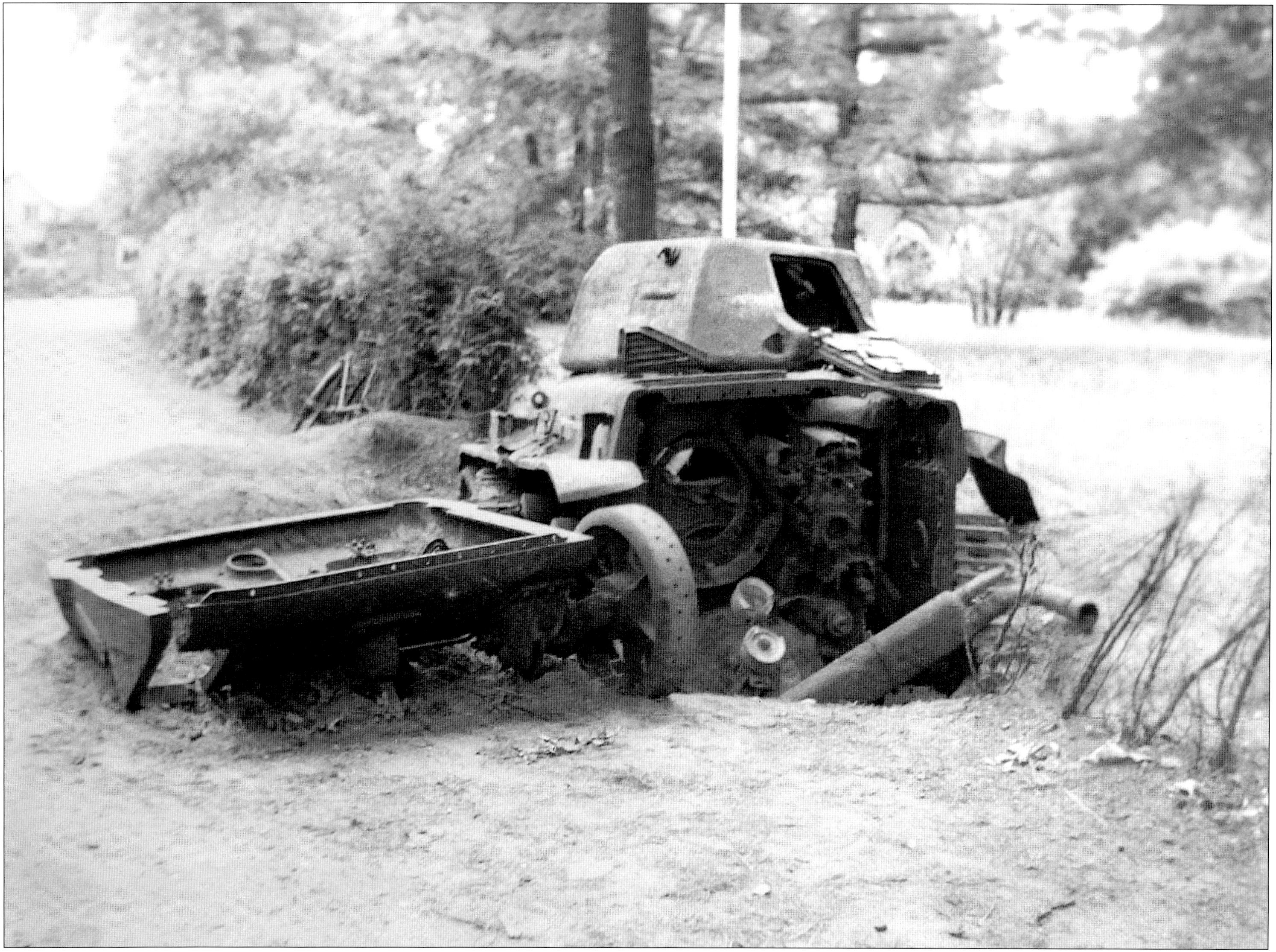

1

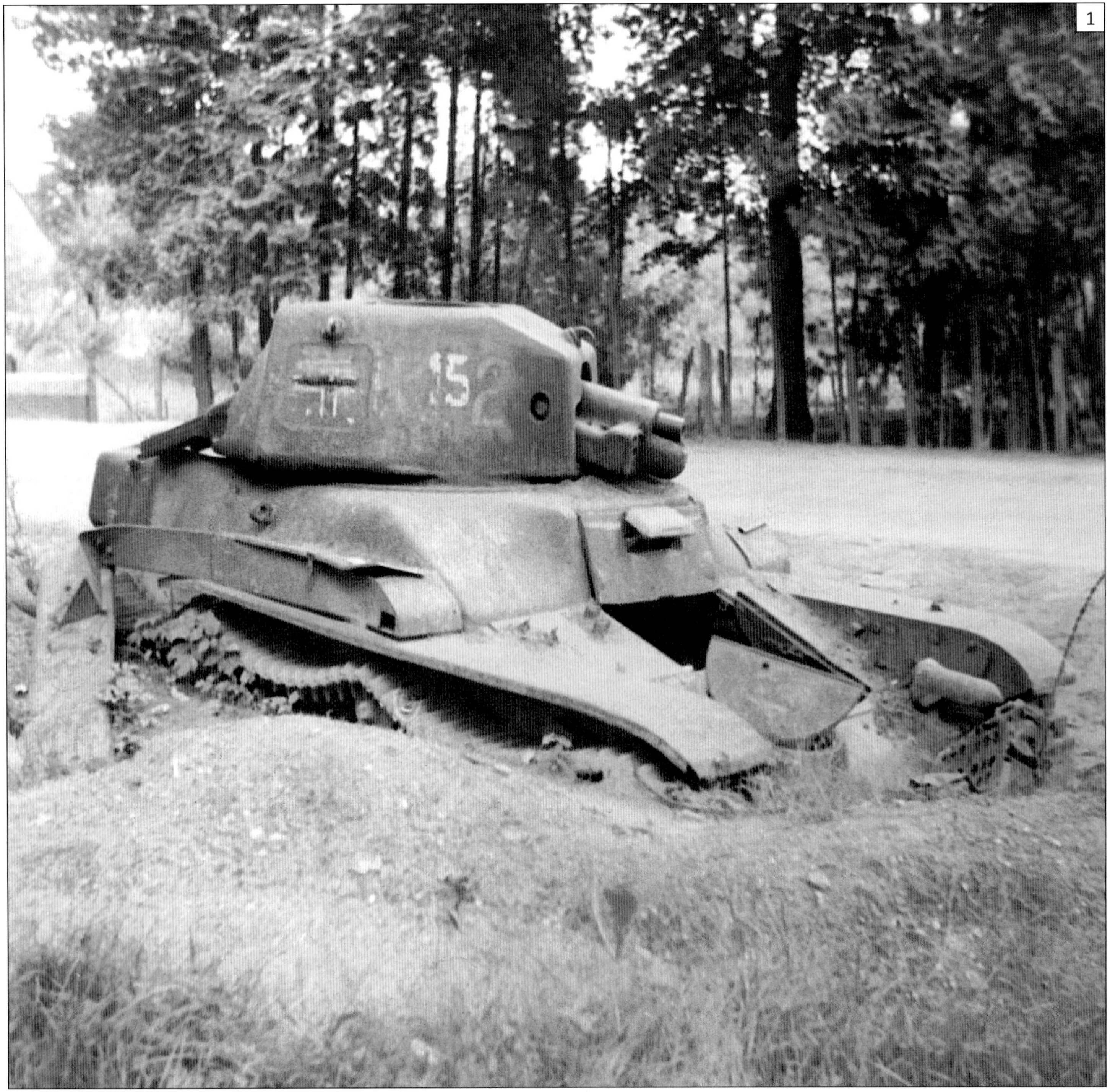

2

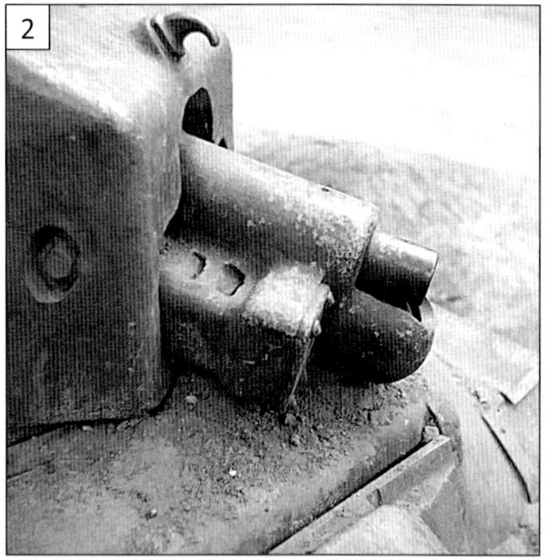

3

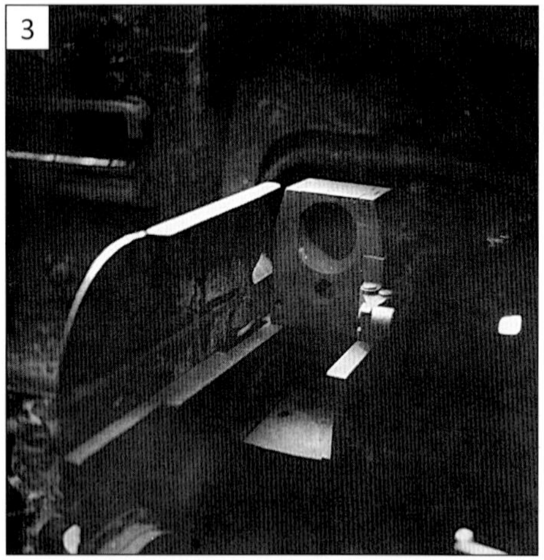

4

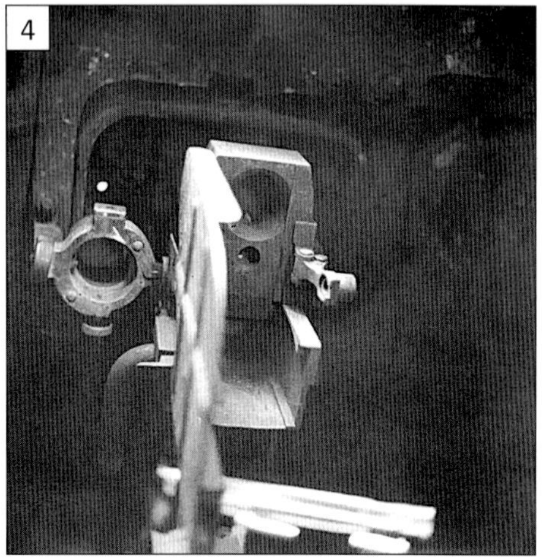

Opposite page: More images of the vehicle shown on the previous pages.
1. The remains of two tactical numbers are starting to fade, as is the 'Balkenkreuz' on the turret visor. The commander's cupola, with its hatch lifted, is sitting on the ground in front of the tank.
2. The extremely short barrel of the 3·7cm L/21 gun
3. Taken from the rear hatch, towards the left, showing the front visor, gun breech and recoil guard.
4. This is pretty much the commander's view, although it has been stripped out. The circular object is the mount for the gunsight. The 7·5mm coaxial MG was fitted to the right of the main gun.

4x LAC

This page: This example, presumably from the same unit, has the tactical number '022' painted in white on the turret side. This is the rear of the vehicle, with its rear plate in the foreground. The force of the explosion has left the top of the superstructure and turret intact, but at a rather jaunty angle.

LAC

This page: The hand over ceremony of a Panther Ausf.D, tactical number '534' by the Polish 1st Armoured Division to the people of Breda on 29 October 1945. The chassis number 210198 identifies it as being from the first series. The tank stands in Wilhelminapark and was restored in 2004. The tank came from the Meppen dump, although who it belonged to is open to speculation. Martin Block has an idea; read our blog to find out more.

4x PISM

Opposite top: 14 October 1944, and according to the cation, a Panther Ausf.G has been knocked out by the US Army Air Corps and stands alone in this field in France. So how to explain the penetration in the right flank?
Opposite bottom: Stills from US Signal Corps motion picture film, which gave the location as Alsace-Serres, France, and the date as 19 October 1944. US tankers inspect the Panther (now with tow cables attached), examine the hole in its flank, and ultimately drive away with their new prize. Ground pressure of the Panther was 0·88kg/sq.cm, allowing it to traverse the muddy field. **Pages 66-67:** At speed on a winding road. The rear view shows the distinctive 'disc' camouflage application. The 'discs' become apparent only if you relax your eyes enough to allow them to 'appear.'

6x NARA

'Disc' Panther at Parroy

'Disc' Panther at Parroy

'Disc' Panther at Parroy

'Disc' Panther at Parroy

Opposite: An M32 ARV follows the Panther closely. By now it becomes apparent that the GI standing in the driver's hatch is not actually driving the tank but probably directing the driver, or kicking him in the back. The driver's hatch itself sits over the radio operator's position and was designed to be removed in an emergency. **This page:** Troops scatter as the Panther wheels into town from the direction of Einville and detours away from Hoéville. Note how much the tank leans as it makes the turn. The location has been confirmed as being Parroy, 5km Southeast of Arracourt, by Fred Carbon and Andrew Hall, and the consensus among Roddy, Matthias and Martin is that our Panther belonged to Panzer-Brigade.113. It was lost on 13th October 1944 when knocked-out by a US M10 tank destroyer. The I./Pz.Lehr-Rgt.130 was attached to Pz.Brig.113 during September 1944 and was destroyed during the battles Northwest of Lunéville.

4x NARA

'Disc' Panther at Parroy

69

8 April 1945, Pvt. T. Romero of the 166th Signal Photo Co. photographed an anti tank gun set up by men of the 6th Armored Division to repel possible counter-attack near Mühlhausen Germany. At left is a knocked out German Pz.Kpfw.IV with no apparent camouflage pattern. Artillery and air power would be called upon in case of attack, as this 57mm Anti tank gun would be hard pressed to stop determined enemy armour.

USAHEC

PFC Vernon B. Fox, of M Company, 376th Infantry Regiment, 94th Infantry Division, got up close and personal with the wreck of a Pz.Kpfw.IV at Volyně, Czechoslovakia. The tank has a faint 6.Panzer-Division insignia on the driver's front plate, just next to the driver's visor. Note how dark the muzzle brake of the gun is in comparison to the rest of the tank. **A.Fox**

If a tree falls in the forest, and nobody hears it, does it still ... This Sturmgeschütz IV has received a treatment of concrete on the front and side of the driver's compartment, perhaps more for psychological reinforcement for the driver than for protection. Even though the front plate of the driver's compartment was 80mm thick, it had a slope of 0°. The superstructure front opposite the driver also had the concrete treatment, in a wedge shape.

R.Kosick

Spare track stands in for concrete on this Sturmgeschütz IV overtaken by GIs of 415th Infantry Regiment, 104th Infantry Division. The data with this photo gives a date of May 1945, but judging by the GI's attire and that bare tree in the background, we rather think it is January or February 1945. An explosive charge has been used to blow the gun in half, rendering it useless.

USAHEC

Panzer IV/70(V) inside and out

Above and below: Two poor photos of two Jagdpanzer IVs from 2./SS-Pz.Jg.Abt.17, 17.SS-Pz.Gren.Div. on Avenue Rubillard, Le Mans, France on 8 August 1944. One was knocked out by a direct hit from a cannon of the US 90th Infantry Division, the other was abandoned by the crew. Fabrice Avoie's *Sarthe, aout 1944 Histoire d'une Libération* gives the tactical numbers as '221' and '222'. This book is an excellent resource for this part of the campaign in France.
2x W.Auerbach

Top and above: A GI snapped these two Panzer IV/70(V)'s that travelled in tandem to this spot in a field and then ... stopped! They later attracted the attention of an Ordnance Technical Intell officer who produced a detailed report on one of them. The vehicles were possibly numbered '1032' and '1037' by Ordnance Evacuation units surveying battlefields for scrap since the numbers don't appear in reports. **Opposite:** Three well known shots showing the low, mean stature of the Panzer IV/70(V).
2x W.Auerbach, 3x NARA

Panzer IV/70(V) inside and out

Panzer IV/70(V) inside and out

Vehicle '1032' was covered in ETO Ordnance Technical Intelligence Report No. 27 dated 6 October 1944. Observations by Lt. George D. Drury. The report gives the chassis number as 340756, this is a typo, as the chassis numbers ran 320001 - 321725, so should be 320756. Normal road wheels appear on the front bogies. These would later be changed to steel resilient road wheels to cope with the vehicle's nose-heaviness. The curved armour plate over the periscopic gunsight aperture on the roof is missing. This plate was not pushed along by the gun sight, but was attached to a separate armature that ran in the much narrower right hand side of the slot.

NARA

Timm Haasler gives us his thoughts on who might have operated these vehicles: "*Since the two tank destroyers carry 'Zimmerit' coatings they must have left the factory in August/September 1944. All Pz. IV/70(V) produced during this time were issued to the newly formed Panzer brigades. These particular two vehicles ended up with either Pz.Brig. 107 or 108, i.e. 4./Pz.Abt. 2107 or 4./Pz.Abt. 2108 respectively. The Pz IV/70 (V) figures for Panzer-Brigade 108 are quite confusing. 4./ Pz.Abt. 2108 reported a total of 8 tanks on 04.10.44 which would have meant a loss of 3 tanks since the brigade had arrived in the West. On 24.10.44 the brigade reported a total of 10 tanks. During that time the remnants of Panzer-Brigade 108 were integrated into 116. Panzer-Division. The next day Pz.Jg.Abt. 228 reported an additional 10 tanks in its inventory which would confirm the tanks reported by Panzer-Brigade 108 the day before, as 4./ 2108 was integrated into Pz.Jg.Abt. 228. I couldn't find any allocations of Pz IV/70 (V) for Panzer-Brigade 108 in October but one never knows if 4./ Pz.Abt. 2108 received some repaired tanks via Panzer-Stützpunkt Nord.*

On the other side it looks like that 4./ Pz.Abt. 2107 lost a total of 5 Pz.IV/70 (V) during its engagement in the Netherlands (Monthly report dated 01.11.44 in combination with BA-MA RH 10/214, page. 51.) A lot is pointing in the direction of 4./ Pz.Abt. 2107.

Right: A view of the roof missing part of the commander's hatch and periscope. Compare to *Panzerwrecks 3,* page 91.

TTM

Panzer IV/70(V) inside and out

Lt. Drury: *"The chassis has a similar appearance to the latest model 7.5cm Stu.K. 40 mounted on the PzKpfw IV chassis. In this model though, the machine gun opening to the left of the driver's vision ports has been dispensed with.* [See Panzerwrecks 8, page 42 for a photo of this feature.] *Top arrangements are the same. Gun is locked in travelling position by yoke pivoting on glacis plate. Yoke is of interest in that it is spring loaded. This allows it to fall out of the way when lock is released by elevating the gun. Armor: Superstructure front 80mm at 50°. Hull: Upper nose plate 80mm at 45°, Lower nose plate 50mm at 55°. Height (to top of periscope shields) 6ft 5ins. Type of construction - all welded with front superstructure plate reinforced by bolting to brackets which in turn are welded to the hull sides."* [See page 81 for this last detail.]

Note the vertical application of 'Zimmerit' under the driver's visor.

Opposite: A photo of enemy ordnance item '1037' showing details of the gun travel lock, driver's visor and conical cover over the MG port. The armour surface around the MG port was left clear of 'Zimmerit' to allow it to open and close smoothly. Note how the towing lug has been strengthened with shaped armour plate. **This page:** No 'Zimmerit' was applied to the lower nose.
2x TTM

Panzer IV/70(V) inside and out

Panzer IV/70(V) inside and out

Left: A view of the gun casement with the mantlet removed revealing the inner armoured 'collar' and shield. **Below:** With mantlet and travel lock in place.

2x TTM

80

Right: Interior of the MG port. The crank below the mount moved the shutter open and closed. 600 rounds were carried for the MG.

Below: The MG port's conical cover. Note the angle iron 'stops' for the cover. *"Subsidiary Armament: Provision for mounting a M.G. in the right front superstructure (probably a 7·92mm M.G. 42) was made. No armament was found with the vehicle however."*

The offset arrangement of the main armament meant the loader was forced into an awkward position against the right sponson to sight and fire his weapon. The tunnel for the drive train and the breech of the gun effectively separated him on the right hand side of the fighting compartment.

2x TTM

Panzer IV/70(V) inside and out

Panzer IV/70(V) inside and out

Lt. Drury: *"In accordance with usual practice, the buffer and recuperator have been mounted on top of the breech and gun tube. A hydro-pneumatic equilibrator is attached to the right side of the gun. To further balance the piece, a cast iron weight measuring 6" x 8-1/4" x 16-5/8" has been added to the rear recoil guard [See page 85.] Of the three vehicles examined, provisions for muzzle brakes had been on two of the tubes while no provision had been made on the other. [Note: the barrels with threads were taken directly from Panther production. No Panzer IV /70 (V) left the factory with a muzzle brake fitted.] Appearance of this tube was similar to our latest 76mm gun as mounted on the Sherman M4 Tank. The compressed air scavenging system as used on the Panther guns has been retained. Power for the small compressor is taken by belt drive from the main propeller shaft. No sights were on the vehicle, but are similar to that of the 7.5 cm. Stu.K. 40. The range drum was calibrated as follows: Pzgr. 39/42: 0 -30; Spgr. 42: 0 - 50."*

The two grab handles over the driver's position assisted him in reaching and leaving his position. He sat with his back against the armoured box protecting the fuel tank.

1x TTM and 1x NARA

Panzer IV/70(V) inside and out

Ammunition racks along the right sponson and a hole for an electric fan in the firewall leading to the engine compartment. (The extraction fan for the gun fumes was in the roof.)

Lt Drury: *"Ammunition: There is stowage for 57 rounds in the fighting compartment. This is stowed 20 rounds to each sponson with 13 rounds stowed horizontally along the left side. 4 rounds are stowed vertically just forward of these rounds. the ammunition carried is the same as that used in the Panther Tank. 30 rounds of A.P.C.B.C. and 21 rounds of H.E. were still in the vehicle."*

This passage in the report causes some confusion because the bulk of the ammunition was supposedly stowed on the right side, split between the sponson and the space under the MG mount, for easy access to the loader. The left side of the fighting compartment was occupied by the driver, gunner and commander, plus the escape hatch in the floor. Lt. Drury may have made a mistake.

Did all this uparmouring and upgunning make practical sense? The short answer is yes, on paper. The Panzerjäger IV carried 79 rounds for the main armament (7·5cm Pak 39 L/48) and could handily defeat the British and American tanks and all but the heaviest Russian tank destroyers before they could close to within 500 metres for a kill. The 7·5 cm Pak 42 L/70 could kill even the heaviest Russian tanks at long range but carried fewer rounds, rounds that would be wasted firing at longer ranges where hits could not be assured.

TTM

Radio racks for the Fu5 and other fittings for the fire extinguisher, etc. Dead centre is the rectangular hatch through which the engine can be seen. Note the counterweight on the end of the recoil guard.

TTM

The lines of this Pz.Sfl.2 für 7·62 Pak 36, with steeply inclined track run, large road wheels and long thin barrel pointing upwards, give the impression of alertness, agility and speed, all attributes of a successful tank hunter. Crews and commanders, however, had a different impression after engaging the enemy, as shortcomings such as pitiful crew protection, high silhouette, high ground pressure, sights that quickly went out of alignment, and high smoke producing propellant quickly made it a battlefield casualty unless employed judiciously. The gun itself was a potent design and, once on target, its rounds could kill most enemy armour easily. The caption gives the location as Fulda.

D.Brown

This GI standing alongside the Sfl. gives an idea of its high silhouette. Successful tactics included opening fire from concealed positions and changing firing positions frequently. Martin Block sheds some light on who used it: "The date is probably 5th April 1945, the date of capture of the town by US troops. Unit has been identified as 2./Panzerjäger-Ersatz- und Ausbildungs-Abteilung.9 / Panzer-Ausbildungs-Verband 'Thüringen' attached to the 2.Panzer-Division. On 27.3.1945, Pz.Jg.Ausb.Abt.9, the combat element, had reached Hünfeld, 16 km NNE of Fulda, with 3x Sf. 7·62cm, 3x Sf. 4·7cm and 1x StuG, while Pz.Jg. Ers.Abt.9 had remained behind to continue to provide replacements."

D.Brown

These two views of '212' shows the gun at maximum depression. Not much armour was available to protect the crew from overhead fire or encircling infantry, and the armour fitted was thin. Coordination and communication between the four man crew was therefore essential for survival, and this crew may have been spared by the cessation of hostilities.

Grease had seeped from the hub caps, rust and streaks had appeared in the paint, and the leaves had returned to shade the park by the time these two photos were taken. Note the gun crutch tucked up under the gun on the opposite page.

1x L.Archer, 1x AMC

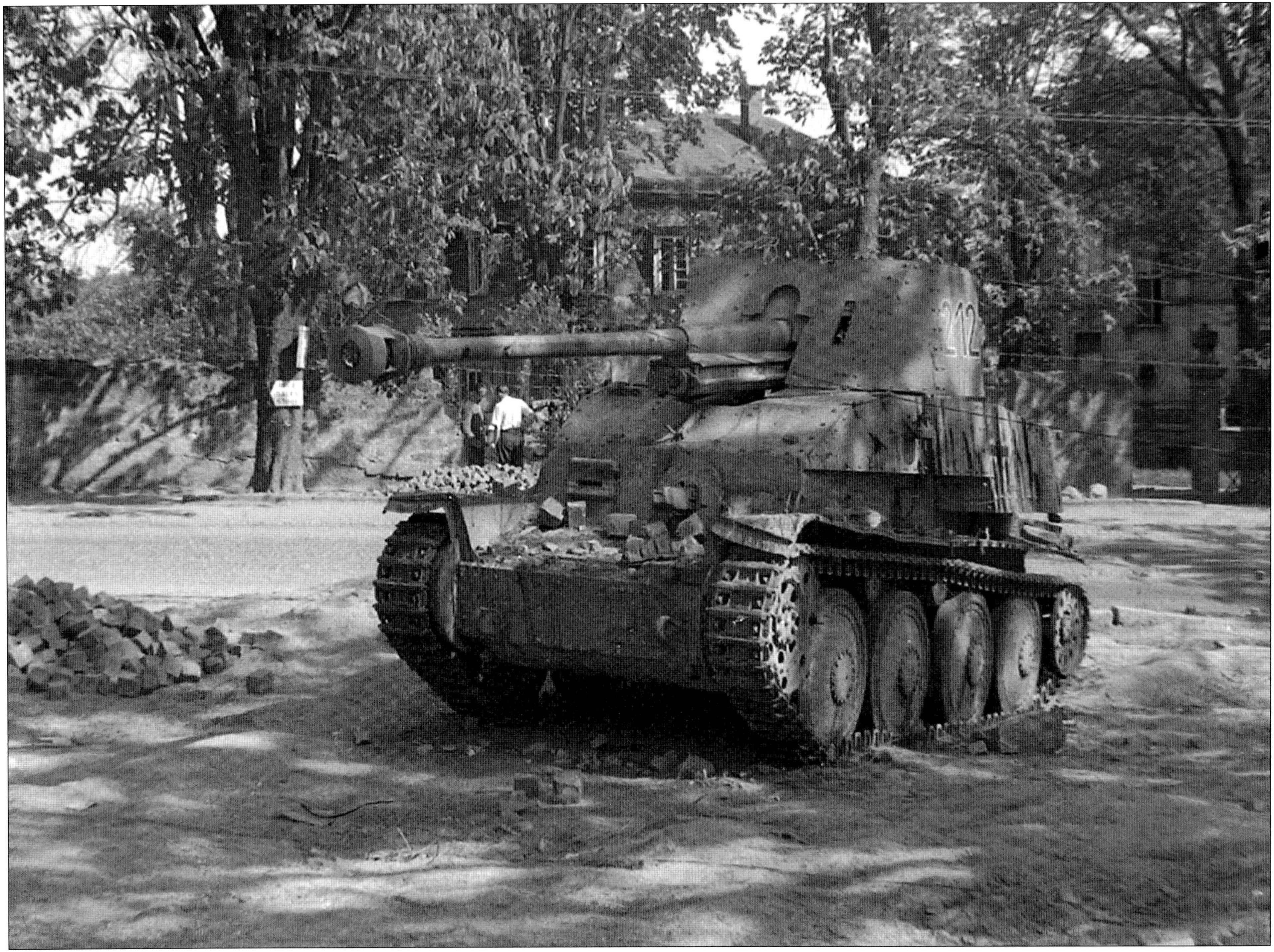
212

Czech menfolk pose with a leichte Schützenpanzerwagen (Sd.Kfz.250) at an unknown location. A round into the engine compartment has shattered the 14·5mm front plate. Something had been fitted to this front plate, as there are the remains of brackets and weld scars. An obscured unit insignia, in the shape of a shield, is just visible.

P.Doležal

Leichter Schützenpanzerwagen (2cm) (SdKfz.250/9) Ausf.A with ten sided turret on 8 May 1945. With the fender and louvred panel missing we can see the muffler arrangement, and this top down view allows us to see the bullet splash rail in front of the turret. The 2cm Kw.K 38 and coax MG34 could be elevated to an impressive 85°. Note the absence of any protective screens over the turret and the bracket for mounting an antenna base at the five o'clock position. Although not an ideal recon vehicle, the le.S.P.W. (2cm) (Sd.Kfz.250/9) was adequate. The number '114' is the tactical number, '462' was added by a US recovery crew.

AMC

18 November 1944, T/3 Jack G. Kitzerow of the 165th Signal Photo Co says about the photo: *"S/1C Jerry Santucci, Bronx NY, examines Thompson sub machine gun which has 2 clips taped together, providing twice as much ammo for quick shooting."*

The weapon system of the m.S.P.W. (Drilling) (Sd.Kfz.251/21) in the background functioned much the same way: the middle gun was used to find the range of the target and then the two outer guns were quickly brought to bear to pour on the firepower. Having three separate sources of ammo readily at hand allowed heavy, sustained, suppressive fire to be laid down with a mixture of different rounds. Note that the S.P.W. is trackless and that the armoured body has separated along the flange behind the driver's cab. In the West by November 1944 these vehicles were to be found in 9. and 116. Pz.Div., 25.Pz.Gren.Div., and Pz.Brig.106.

NARA

A mittlerer Schützenpanzerwagen Ausf.C (riveted) with an armoured body produced by Bohemia, Böhm Leipa. The headlight appears to be non-standard. With the Ausf.C, the turn signals were relocated from being in front of the side visors to a position behind the armoured cowl on the engine compartment. An antenna base is located on the roof over the co-driver's position. The MP and his friend in the officer's hat appear to be inside the vehicle, but we still don't know what the 'roof' is made of; it could be the standard 'Verdeck' canvas cover-over-bows anchored with wood along the sides, or, more likely, sheet metal, or a combination of all three.

W.Auerbach

Backs are turned on a burnt out mittlerer Schützenpanzerwagen (Sd.Kfz.251) Ausf.D as if to signify its irrelevance. Only a pair of boots behind the vehicle shows anyone is paying attention to it. One of the 'Spriegeln' (metal bows used to support the canvas cover) arches over the scorched crew compartment. This vehicle, which has the flat visors, may have stood guard in front of an administrative building at one time.

VHU

Photos taken by Paul Toth of 771st Tank Battalion. **Top Left:** GIs investigate a Tiger II knocked out near Kassel, Germany. **Top Right:** A G.I. climbs on the rear of the Tiger as Toth stands back to photograph the penetrations in the right side of the turret. **Left:** In this photo, we can see that the Tiger II is located just off a road, which is probably why it was photographed in the first place. Matthias Radu gives us a bit more about this wreck: *"This example, probably the very last from the line, had been taken directly from the Henschel factory at Kassel to a small road near an open field east of the A7 Autobahn exit Kassel-Ost, adjacent to the eastern ramp of Dresdner Strasse / Kasseler Strasse bridge across the motorway leading towards Heiligenrode and Niestetal, east of Kassel, Germany. There, it had been knocked-out by an US tank destroyer, probably from C Co, 702nd Tank Destroyer Bn. Story goes that locals had told the GIs a way around the Tiger which enabled them to take it out from behind. According to Kleine/Kühne, the driver of the Tiger, Rudi Kaiser, was killed. Since he had been on the roster of 3./schwere Panzer-Abteilung.511, that is the most likely candidate for the unit it belonged to. Date of loss should be 5th April 1945."*

2x M.Toth, 1x USAHEC

The Tiger II was among the last produced before the factory was overrun in late March 1945. It had single link tracks and 18-tooth drive sprockets, and the aperture for the gun sight had a pronounced 'U' shaped rain guard welded over it. It was finished in a base coat of Dunkelgrün (RAL 6003) oversprayed with Dunkelgelb.(RAL 7028). This Tiger had transport tracks fitted, a common feature of the last batch of Tiger II's issued to 3./s.Pz.Abt.510 and 3./s.Pz.Abt.511. Note the pock marking from small arms fire around the hull MG, the missing headlight, and lack of foliage loops on the turret.

D.Brown